GAL
CENGA(

D0232914

Drama for Students, Volume 27

Project Editor: Sara Constantakis Rights Acquisition and Management: Mardell Glinski Schultz, Barb McNeil, Tracie Richardson, Robyn Young Composition: Evi Abou-El-Seoud Manufacturing: Drew Kalasky

Imaging: John Watkins

Product Design: Pamela A. E. Galbreath, Jennifer Wahi Content Conversion: Katrina Coach Product Manager: Meggin Condino © 2010 Gale, Cengage Learning

For product information and technology assistance, contact us at **Gale Customer Support, 1-800-877-4253.**

For permission to use material from this text or product, submit all requests online at **www.cengage.com/permissions.**

Further permissions questions can be emailed to **permissionrequest@cengage.com** While every effort has been made to ensure the reliability of the information presented in this publication, Gale, a part of Cengage Learning, does not guarantee the accuracy of the data contained herein. Gale accepts no payment for listing; and inclusion in the publication of any organization, agency, institution, publication, service, or individual does not imply endorsement of the editors or publisher. Errors brought to the attention of the publisher and verified to the satisfaction of the publisher will be corrected in future editions.

Gale
27500 Drake Rd.
Farmington Hills, MI, 48331-3535

ISBN-13: 978-0-7876-8123-4
ISBN-10: 0-7876-8123-7

ISSN 1094-9232

This title is also available as an e-book.

ISBN-13: 978-1-4144-4939-5
ISBN-10: 1-4144-4939-9
Contact your Gale, a part of Cengage Learning sales
representative for ordering information.

Printed in the United States of America
1 2 3 4 5 6 7 14 13 12 11 10

A Streetcar Named Desire

Tennessee Williams

1951

Introduction

A Streetcar Named Desire is a film released in 1951, based on the play of the same title by Tennessee Williams, which was first produced in 1947. The film is closely based on the play. It is set in a poor section of New Orleans and features four main characters: Blanche DuBois; her sister, Stella; Stella's husband, Stanley Kowalski; and Mitch, a friend of Stanley's. Blanche comes to stay with Stella and Stanley in their cramped apartment. Blanche, a refined but unhappy woman who has been unable to find lasting love, soon comes into conflict with the blunt-spoken and aggressive Stanley. She is briefly courted by Mitch, but the new love does not last, and Blanche ends up losing touch with reality and being sent to an asylum for the insane.

The film was the first ever to win three Academy Awards (also known as Oscars) for acting. British actress Vivien Leigh won the award for Best Actress for her portrayal of Blanche. Kim Hunter as Stella and Karl Malden as Mitch won Oscars for Best Supporting Actress and Best Supporting Actor, and Elia Kazan won in the Best Director category. However, Marlon Brando, whose brilliant performance as Stanley has thrilled moviegoers for over half a century, was not rewarded with an Oscar.

With its ruthless presentation of love and loneliness and its stellar individual performances, *A Streetcar Named Desire* is regarded as one of the best American films ever made. Some of the content of the film was considered controversial at the time, and viewers should be aware that some scenes contain intense confrontations between the characters, although the actual violence shown is minimal.

FILM TECHNIQUE

Black-and-White Film

The film was shot in black and white, and it uses lighting to bring out one of the motifs of the play: Blanche's desire to present herself only in dim light out of fear that daylight would reveal her true age. Symbolically, Blanche's desire for darkness over light suggests her need to maintain illusions at the expense of truth. She keeps her room dark, as in the scene in which she meets Mitch, which takes place half in shadow. It is as if there is a veil spread over Blanche. Mitch has to light a match so that she can read the inscription on the cigarette case he shows her. She then asks Mitch to place a colored paper lantern over the bare bulb in her room, to soften the light, before she will switch it on.

The artful use of lighting to convey this aspect of Blanche's personality occurs again in the scene in which Mitch comes late at night and accuses her of lying to him (chapter 20 in the DVD selections). Blanche's face is half in shadow when she hears the doorbell ringing. The film then cuts to the empty and dark living room, which is partially lit by a flashing neon sign out in the street, suggesting the insistent, harsh light that Blanche tries so hard to keep at bay. ("I like the dark. The dark is comforting to me," she says later in this scene.) The light from the flashing neon sign continues as she lets

Mitch in and at intervals during the scene. When Mitch switches one light on, Blanche gives a little gasp and runs for cover like a frightened animal. Mitch rips the lantern off the bulb, and she begs him not to turn the bare bulb on. He cruelly forces her to stand with her face directly under the light so he can see what she is really like. It is a savage moment, symbolically as well as physically. The harsh light of reality is like poison to her, and as she confesses what she has been through in her life and why, the scene plays out in normal lighting. The illusion she tried to preserve is gone, and with it anything that gives her hope. When she returns from the street after following Mitch out, she rushes around, closing the shutters to keep out all the light from the street and turning off all the lights again, as if by doing so she could go back to her comforting world of illusion. Again, her face is seen more than half in shadow. The lighting tells Blanche's story, reinforcing the message conveyed by the words.

Duration of Shots

The length of a shot can also create various effects. In moments when the action moves fast, the shots will tend to be of shorter duration. This technique of quick cutting conveys a sense of dynamism and motion. The pace of the film suddenly picks up. An example is the chaotic scene after Stanley throws the radio out of the window, angrily chases after Blanche, and is pulled back by the other men. As in real life, the eye of the viewer must move quickly to take in such a scene and see who is doing what to whom. Confusion abounds. In contrast, some of the many close-ups in the film are of longer duration; the action slows, and the emotions of the characters are explored. The variation in pace creates the subtle rhythm of the film, in which scenes of reflection and emotional disclosure are followed by explosions of action and movement.

Plot Summary

The film *A Streetcar Named Desire* begins at a railroad station in New Orleans. Blanche DuBois emerges from the crowd, not sure where to go. She asks directions from a young man who tells her that the streetcar she needs, named Desire, is approaching. She boards the streetcar and arrives at a lively area of the city, where people are out enjoying themselves. She asks a woman for directions to a street called Elysian Fields and is told that she is in it. The woman is Eunice, who lives upstairs in the same building as Blanche's sister, Stella. Stella and her husband, Stanley Kowalski, occupy the downstairs apartment.

The film cuts to a bowling alley, where Stella is watching Stanley play. Blanche finds Stella and they embrace. Stella points out her husband, who is seen stirring up a quarrel involving several men. Blanche says she does not want to meet him just yet. They find a quiet corner, and Blanche, who is a schoolteacher, explains that she has been able to come during the school term because the superintendent suggested she take a leave of absence. She was suffering from nervous exhaustion.

The next sequence begins in the Kowalskis' apartment, where Stella is running a bath for Blanche. Stella makes a place for Blanche in the small apartment. Blanche is distressed and needs to have people around her. She asks whether Stanley will like her, and Stella replies that they will get along well; it is clear that Stella and Stanley are in love.

Blanche reproaches Stella for leaving their home in Mississippi and going to New Orleans, while Blanche stayed at Belle Reve, their home, trying to keep it going. This was a burden on her, especially when their parents died. Blanche had to manage on her small teacher's salary, and now the house has been lost. Distressed, Stella runs to another room.

The film cuts to the street, where Stanley returns with his friends Mitch and Steve. Steve quarrels with his wife, Eunice. Blanche introduces herself to the muscular Stanley, who is wearing a tight-fitting, sweat-soaked T-shirt. Stanley offers a drink, but she says (untruthfully) that she rarely drinks. After asking Blanche whether she minds, Stanley removes his shirt and puts on a clean one. As they chat, Stanley discovers that Blanche is going to be staying there. Blanche seems nervous, and Stanley says he guesses she will find him an unrefined character. He also says he was told she had been married once, a remark that upsets Blanche. She says her husband died, and she is troubled by the memory.

In the next scene, Stanley arrives in the apartment with Blanche's trunk. While Blanche is in the bath, Stella tells Stanley her sister is upset over losing the family home. Stanley wants to see documents regarding the sale. Stella knows nothing about it, but Stanley gets angry. He says that under the Napoleonic law that operates in Louisiana, anything that belongs to a wife also belongs to the husband, and he feels that she may have been swindled, which means he has been swindled, too.

He pulls out some expensive-looking clothes from Blanche's trunk, saying that Blanche could never have bought such things on a teacher's salary. Over Stella's protests, he says he will get an expert to appraise the value of the clothes. Then he finds Blanche's jewelry, and says he will get that appraised as well. Exasperated, Stella goes outside to the porch.

Blanche emerges from the bathroom. Going behind the curtain that cordons off her sleeping area, she is disturbed when she sees the ransacked trunk. When she has put on another dress, she asks Stanley to fasten the buttons at the back. Stanley questions her about the stylish clothes, and she says they were gifts from long ago. She keeps trying to get Stanley to compliment her on her appearance, without success. He gets impatient with her attempted flattery and yells at her, which brings Stella in from the porch. Blanche sends her away.

Stanley explains to Blanche about the Napoleonic code, and Blanche insists she has never cheated anyone. She retrieves a box from her trunk, in which she keeps most of her papers. She also pulls out what she says are love letters, and Stanley grabs them. She snatches at them and they get scattered on the floor. She gathers them up, saying they are from her dead husband. Then she gives

Stanley the legal papers relating to Belle Reve. She says that several generations of the family squandered their wealth until all that was left was the house and twenty acres of land. Stanley says he will have a lawyer examine them. He also reveals that Stella is pregnant. When Stella returns, Blanche congratulates her and says she smoothed things over with Stanley.

Stella and Blanche go out to dinner, while Stanley's friends Mitch, Steve, and Pablo arrive for a game of poker. The gathering goes on until late at night, and Eunice, Steve's wife, bangs on the ceiling (the floor of their apartment), trying to get him to come home. Steve takes no notice. The men move the table before Eunice can start pouring boiling water through the cracks in the ceiling.

When Stella and Blanche return, Stanley is irritated by their presence and suggests that they go up to see Eunice. He slaps her rear in front of the other men, which angers her. Blanche meets Mitch outside the bathroom, and after Mitch goes to join the other men, Blanche tells Stella that he seems a cut above the others. Blanche inquires further, and Stella tells her that Mitch is single and works in the spare parts company. It is the same company Stanley works for, but Stella says Stanley has a better job.

As Stella passes on gossip about Eunice, the two women laugh. Stanley complains about the noise and then complains again when Blanche switches on the radio. Angry, he comes into Blanche's room and switches it off himself.

Mitch quits the card game, and he and Blanche engage in conversation. Mitch is charmed by Blanche, and she, craving attention, is pleased to accept his interest. She asks him to put a colored paper lantern that she has just purchased over the light bulb. Then she turns the radio on again and waltzes to the music, while Mitch self-consciously imitates her and a bemused Stella looks on.

Furious at the noise, Stanley rushes in, grabs the radio, and hurls it through the window. An angry Stella tries to throw the other men out, and there is a commotion. Stanley chases after Stella and has to be restrained by the other men. Pablo hits him, knocking him unconscious. The men drag him to the shower and put his head under it; the cold water revives him. There is another scuffle as Stanley throws the men off.

Stanley calls out for Stella, who has fled upstairs with Blanche. When he cannot find her, he sobs. He stands outside the building and calls up to Stella to come back. Eunice yells abuse at Stanley, but Stella cannot stay away for long. She returns, and they share a passionate embrace. Contrite, he carries her back to their apartment.

Terrified by the altercation, Blanche descends to the now quiet street, where she encounters Mitch, who tells her not to be frightened because Stanley and Stella are very much in love. Blanche thanks him for being kind.

In the morning, Blanche returns to the apartment. Stella is in bed alone; Stanley has already left to get the car fixed. Blanche goes to comfort her sister, only to discover that Stella is not bothered by the events of the previous night. Stanley has always smashed things, she says. Blanche does not understand why her sister accepts this behavior, and she has a plan for both of them to escape. Stella tells Blanche she does not want to escape her marriage. Outside, the returning Stanley overhears all this. Blanche complains to Stella that Stanley is common, like an animal, with his crude desires. Stella is unmoved by Blanche's criticisms of her husband, but she embraces her sister tenderly. Stanley enters, having overheard every word. Stella rushes to him, and they embrace, while Stanley grins at Blanche.

Eunice is chased down the fire escape by Steve. She shouts that he hit her and she is going to call the police. As Stanley comes in, though, he says she went to the bar first for a drink.

Stanley says he has heard something about Blanche from a man named Shaw, who says he met her in the Hotel Flamingo in her hometown. Unsettled, Blanche replies that the Flamingo is not the sort of place where she would be seen.

After Stanley leaves, Blanche asks Stella what people have been saying about her. She reveals there was some unsavory gossip about her in Auriol, her hometown (called Laurel in the play). Stella gives Blanche a Coke with a shot of whiskey, and Blanche promises Stella she will not be staying long. Blanche is distressed, and some of the drink gets spilled on her dress.

Blanche has been dating Mitch, and he is coming for her at seven that night. Blanche wants to hold Mitch's interest and eventually marry him so she will not have to stay with Stella and Stanley any longer. Stella comforts her.

Blanche is on her own in the house when a young man arrives, collecting money for the evening newspaper. Blanche flirts with him, even kissing him. As the boy leaves, Mitch arrives, carrying roses for Blanche.

Mitch and Blanche dance at an amusement park on the lake. They go outside and talk on the pier, and Mitch asks permission to kiss her. He makes it plain that he likes her a lot. Blanche laughs out of embarrassment. She lights a candle and they sit down at a table. Mitch is proud of how he keeps himself physically fit. He says he weighs 207 pounds and asks her what she weighs. She lets him pick her up and he remarks on how light she is. When he puts her down he tries to kiss her, but she resists, saying she is old-fashioned in that respect. It is an awkward moment, and Mitch is disappointed. The talk gets around to Stanley, and Mitch says he thinks Stanley does not understand her. Blanche says she thinks he hates her.

As they walk together, Mitch asks her how old she is. He says his mother, who is dying, wants him to settle down, and she wanted to know Blanche's age. The talk turns to loneliness, and Blanche reveals that her husband, whom she married when she was very young, was a sensitive, troubled young man who committed suicide. When they were at a dance one night, he stepped outside and shot himself. Moved by her story, Mitch says they are both lonely. He hopes they can have a life together. Blanche is touched, and they kiss.

The next scene begins in the factory, where several men are restraining Mitch, who wants to attack Stanley. Mitch is forced to calm down.

Later, as Stella and Blanche prepare for Blanche's birthday party, Stanley tells Stella he has found out the details of Blanche's disreputable life in Auriol. She used to live at the sleazy Flamingo Hotel but even that hotel asked her to leave. Stella tries to defend her sister, but Stanley insists he is correct. He says everyone in Auriol regarded Blanche as crazy. He adds that she did not take a leave of absence from her school; she was fired because she became involved with a seventeen-year-old boy. Stanley also tells Stella that Mitch will not be coming to the birthday party, because Stanley has told him about Blanche.

Blanche emerges, fresh after her bath, and knows right away that something is wrong because of the look on Stella's face.

At the birthday supper, Blanche says this is the first time she has ever been stood up, and she starts to tells a joke. She is interrupted by a doorbell ringing upstairs. Then Stella criticizes Stanley for his table manners, which angers Stanley so much that he tells her never to talk like that to him again. He sweeps his cup and saucer to the floor while the two women look down at the table. After he goes outside, Blanche tells Stella she has guessed why Mitch did not come.

Outside, Stella reproaches Stanley for his behavior. Stanley says things will be better when Blanche is gone. Back in the kitchen, Stanley becomes angry again because Blanche calls him a Polack. Stanley then presents Blanche with what he says is a birthday gift. It is an envelope containing a bus ticket to Auriol for the following Tuesday. Blanche is upset and runs to the bathroom. Once again, Stella rebukes Stanley for his cruelty. Stanley explains that they were happy until Blanche arrived. Stella then feels her baby move and tells Stanley to take her to the hospital.

Blanche is alone when she hears knocking at the door. It is Mitch, who is agitated and speaks roughly to her. When she offers him a drink he refuses, adding that he has been told by Stanley that she has been drinking excessively all summer. Still aggressive, Mitch switches the light on, saying he has never seen her in daylight and has therefore never had a good look at her. Blanche prefers dim lighting, which helps her conceal her age. He sees she is older than he thought she was but says he does not mind that. What he does mind are the stories he has been told about her life. Blanche admits she has had encounters with men she barely knew. She says it was because she was lonely after her husband's suicide. She needed some protection. Mitch is angry and accuses her of lying to him while they were developing their relationship. Blanche protests that she was sincere.

A blind Mexican woman comes to the door selling flowers for the dead. Blanche is upset because the mention of death reminds her of all the deaths of relatives she endured at Belle Reve. Mitch embraces her, and they kiss. She ask him to marry her, but he says he no longer wants to. She tells him to get out, and she follows him, in a scene added to the film that does not appear in the play, screaming into the street. A few men show concern for her, but she rushes back into the house, closing the shutters and turning the lights off. A police officer is called. He hammers on the door, but Blanche refuses to open it. Later, she dresses up in her finest clothes and retreats into a fantasy world of her own.

Stanley returns from the hospital, saying the baby will not arrive until the morning. Blanche lies that she has received an invitation by telegram from an old flame inviting her to join him on a Caribbean cruise. Stanley knows she is lying but goes along with her for a while. Blanche pretends her wealthy friend is a gentleman who wants her not for an affair but for companionship. She also lies that Mitch asked her to forgive him.

Stanley confronts Blanche with her lies, saying he knew from the beginning what she was like. He pushes her down onto the bed and yells at her, and then he storms out of the room. In desperation, Blanche gathers up some clothes and goes outside, but when she sees the Mexican woman again she returns to the house. She tries to make a phone call to get some help, but Stanley emerges from the bathroom and she breaks off the call. Stanley becomes aggressive, and Blanche runs into her bedroom. Stanley follows. Blanche, believing herself to be in danger, grabs a bottle, breaks it on a table and holds it up to him, trying to keep him at bay. He wrests the bottle top from her, and the film cuts to a shattered mirror.

Some time passes. Eunice is looking after Stella's baby while Stanley and his friends are playing cards. Stella tells Eunice she has made arrangements for Blanche to rest in the country, but Blanche still talks about the cruise she is going on. Blanche emerges from the bathroom, and the two women speak gently to her. Blanche is lost in her fantasy world.

A doctor and nurse arrive from a mental institution. When Blanche hears she has a visitor, she thinks it must be the man who is taking her on the cruise. When she sees him, she says he is not the man she has been expecting. She becomes hysterical and collapses on the floor, while the nurse grips her. Mitch is angry and aims a punch at Stanley; the other men pull him away.

The nurse lets go of Blanche, and the doctor takes Blanche's arm and leads her away. Blanche still does not know who he is. Stella speaks sharply to Stanley, telling him never to touch her again. Blanche is driven away in a car. As Stella holds her baby, she says to herself that she is not going back to Stanley. Off-screen, Stanley calls out her name.

The film stays close to the play, although there are a few changes in location, especially at the beginning. This was done in order to open out the movie beyond the simple stage setting of the play, in which the action takes place almost entirely in the Kowalski apartment. The play opens with Stanley returning home, bringing his wife some meat, which he tosses to her. This scene is omitted from the film, which begins by showing Blanche's arrival at the railroad station in New Orleans. Blanche is then directed by Eunice to the bowling alley, where she meets up with Stella and sees Stanley for the first time. In the play, there is no scene set in the bowling alley. Another change occurs in scene 6 of the play, in which Blanche and Mitch are seen returning to the apartment from their evening together. In the film, they are shown during the evening, first dancing together and then going outside the hall to the pier at the lake, where they talk.

Characters

Blanche DuBois

Blanche DuBois (Vivien Leigh) is an old-fashioned Southern belle who comes from an aristocratic family in Mississippi that has fallen on hard times. She married when she was very young, and her husband, whom she refers to as a "boy," committed suicide. His death still haunts her many years later. After the death of her husband she was never to find love again. She stayed on, a tormented widow, at the family home of Belle Reve, while her family squandered what was left of their wealth and her sister escaped to New Orleans. Blanche survived by taking a job as a teacher of English at a high school, but by this time she was emotionally spent, a fragile, brittle, lonely woman with no one to love and no real purpose to her life. Desperate for love and attention, something to nourish her heart, she started to go downhill, living at a sleazy hotel and entertaining men, always seeking love but never finding it.

The nostalgic Blanche tries to live in a world of high ideals, romance, refinement, and beauty that never really existed, She has fallen in the eyes of the world, but she still thinks of herself as being a member of a higher social class. She lives in a world of nostalgia and illusion. She knows that her beauty is fading, and she desperately wants to reclaim some of the magic of life that she once knew. She needs someone to protect her. By the time she arrives at the home of her sister, she is almost beyond hope. She has been fired from her job as a schoolteacher for having an inappropriate relationship with a seventeen-year-old boy, and she has nowhere else to go. She drinks too much in an effort to blot out the reality of her life, and she still likes to dress in fine clothes and act like the lady she believes she still is. She tries to cover up her past. From the moment she first encounters Stanley, they are in conflict; the longer she stays in the Kowalski apartment, the worse the tension between them grows. After the failure of her brief courtship with Mitch and after Stanley's assault on her, the discrepancy between what she needs and what she is able to get becomes too great, and she slips into madness. The only place left for her is the mental asylum. One of the great tragic figures in American drama, Blanche is an example of a woman who is too emotionally delicate to survive in a world that is populated by men such as Stanley Kowalski.

Vivien Leigh won an Academy Award for Best Actress for her portrayal of Blanche.

Doctor

The doctor (Richard Garrick), an elderly man in a dark suit, comes with the nurse to the Kowalski home to escort Blanche to the mental institution. He treats her gently and offers her his arm as they walk out. Blanche does not know who he is, but she is willing to go with him.

Eunice

Eunice (Peg Hillias) is Steve's wife. She and her husband live in the apartment above the Kowalskis'. Eunice is a forthright woman who knows how to stand up for herself. Steve appears not to treat her very well, but she is unbowed. When the card game downstairs goes on too late, she bangs on the ceiling to get Steve to come home. Then she heats up some boiling water in order to pour it down the cracks in the ceiling. The men know what is coming—she has obviously done this before. On one occasion Eunice rushes out of the house saying her husband has hit her and she is going to call the police, but she never does and is soon reconciled to her husband. However, Eunice has no illusions about the way men are. She appears to dislike Stanley and is not intimidated by him. She gets along well with Stella, looking after the baby, and also speaks kindly to Blanche when Blanche is confused and about to be sent away. Eunice adopts a stoic attitude to life. Whatever has to be endured must be endured. "Life has got to go on," she says near the end of the film. "No matter what happens, you've got to keep on going."

Stanley Kowalski

Stanley Kowalski (Marlon Brando) is Stella's husband. He is between twenty-eight and thirty years old. In World War II he was a master sergeant in the Engineers' Corp, according to Stella, who met him when he was still in uniform. His family is of Polish origin, but he resents it when Blanche brings that up. He prides himself on being an American. Tennessee Williams included the following description of Stanley in the first scene of the stage play:

> Animal joy in his being is implicit in all his movements and attitudes. Since earliest manhood the center of his life has been pleasure with women … not with weak indulgence, dependently, but with the power and pride of a richly feathered male bird among hens.

Stanley is a coarse man; he takes his male superiority for granted and does not accept any challenges to his authority from his wife or Blanche. He drinks and eats with relish and enjoys robust male company. He genuinely loves Stella in his own way and is reduced to sobbing and pleading with her when she flees upstairs to escape him after one of his aggressive outbursts. In that sense he relies on Stella and the love she offers, even though he would probably never admit it or even realize it.

Stanley often takes his aggression out on things rather than people—such as the radio, which he smashes. However, he also can be cruel to others, both mentally and physically. Giving Blanche a bus ticket home as a birthday present is an example of this cruelty. It is like twisting a knife in her heart. Another example of his cruelty is when they are alone in the apartment and he steps over the line and attacks her.

From Stanley's point of view, Blanche represents an intrusion on his happy life with Stella. He can no more understand her than he could understand a cat. She cannot understand him, either, or what Stella would see in him. Stella, however, likes a man who is not afraid to be a man, and that is Stanley Kowalski. He lives his life without reflecting on it, quite unlike Blanche, who is always looking back and wanting life to be something it is not. That would never occur to Stanley. He enjoys the things that life brings him—women, cars, buddies to play poker with, a bottle of beer—and he makes no apology for who he is.

Marlon Brando had played Stanley in the original Broadway play production. This was one of his first film roles. Utterly convincing as Stanley, he made a huge impact on moviegoers. Although the main character in the play is meant to be Blanche, Brando's performance as Stanley was so powerful and riveting that it almost became his film rather than Vivien Leigh's as Blanche. Ever since the film was released, few people can imagine the part of Stanley without seeing Brando in his tight-fitting T-shirt, all muscles and raw masculine power. Countless stage actors since have played the role as, in effect, lesser imitations of Brando.

Stella Kowalski

Stella Kowalski (Kim Hunter) is Stanley

Kowalski's wife and Blanche's sister. Blanche pretends that Stella is older, but in fact Stella is younger by about five years. Stella left the family home in Mississippi to move to New Orleans, where she married Stanley. Blanche resents the fact that Stella left their home, leaving her to cope, but Stella has no regrets. She is happily married to Stanley. She loves him, in spite of his bullying and violent temper and despite the fact that he comes from a lower social class than she does. Although sometimes she becomes angry with his crude behavior, in general she does not mind his aggressive nature; in fact, she even admires it because it shows his masculinity. To Stella, a quarrel with Stanley does not mean much; they soon make up, and she knows that in spite of all his boorishness, he loves her. Blanche does not understand how Stella could want to remain in such a marriage, but Stella does not aspire to Blanche's refined, romantic ideas. She is happy where she is, with what she has. It is true that at the end of the film, she swears she will never go back to Stanley because of the way he treated Blanche, but the audience has seen her return to Stanley before after a quarrel, so her protestations that the marriage is over are less than convincing. In the play, Stella and Stanley embrace at the end, leaving no doubt about the nature of their relationship, whatever shocks it has gone through following Blanche's arrival.

Kim Hunter won an Academy Award for Best Supporting Actress for her portrayal of Stella.

Mexican Woman

The Mexican woman (Edna Thomas) is a blind woman who sells flowers to be displayed at funerals and other occasions. Blanche is upset on both occasions when she sees the Mexican woman because she is reminded of death.

Harold "Mitch" Mitchell

Mitch (Karl Malden) is an old friend of Stanley's. They fought in World War II together. Like Stanley, Mitch is about twenty-eight to thirty years old, and he works in the spare parts department at the same factory that employs Stanley. A bachelor, Mitch looks after his dying mother. When he first meets Blanche, he is quite taken with her, and they go out together several times. Treating her with a gentlemanly courtesy, he accepts Blanche at face value as a refined, attractive woman. He says he has never met anyone like her before. Like Blanche, Mitch is lonely, and he thinks the two of them might be able to succeed together. However, all those hopes are dashed when Stanley tells him the stories about Blanche's past. Mitch does not believe the stories until he verifies them for himself. He fails to show up at Blanche's birthday party, but he comes by later and harangues her for not being honest with him. She still hopes that they can marry, but he says he is no longer interested. "You're not clean enough to bring in the house with my mother," are his final words to her.

Karl Malden won an Academy Award for Best

Supporting Actor for his portrayal of Mitch.

Nurse

The nurse (Ann Dere) is a middle-aged, severe-looking woman who comes with the doctor to take Blanche to the mental institution. She takes charge of Blanche physically, pinning her arms, and asks the doctor whether they will need a straightjacket.

Pablo

Pablo (Nick Dennis) is a friend of Stanley's and a member of the poker-playing group. In the commotion that follows Stanley's tossing of the radio out of the window, Pablo punches Stanley, but Stanley seems to bear him no ill-will for his action. Near the end of the film, Pablo, along with Steve, stares reproachfully at Stanley because of his bad treatment of Blanche.

Steve

Steve (Rudy Bond) is Eunice's husband and Stanley's friend. Like Stanley, he is a rough-hewn character who often argues with his wife. On one occasion, he is seen chasing her down the fire escape, and she runs away, saying that he hit her and she is going to call the police. Later, however, Steve is shown walking Eunice home with his arm around her. He knows how far he can go and what he has to do to win her back.

Young Collector

The young collector (Wright King) is a young man who comes to the Kowalski apartment collecting newspaper money. He is a shy, respectful individual. He refuses Blanche's offer of a drink because he is not allowed to drink while he is working. Blanche flirts with him and kisses him on the mouth.

Since the film is a very close adaptation of the play, all the characters in the play appear in the film. Their personalities and their interactions with one another remain for the most part the same as they are in the play. The only significant change is Stella's less forgiving attitude toward Stanley at the end.

Themes

Loneliness

Blanche arrives in New Orleans without a friend in the world other than her sister, Stella. This is particularly unfortunate for her since she is not the independent type. She needs people, and more especially, she needs love and intimacy in her life. Without it she is helpless and vulnerable. In New Orleans, though, she is an outsider. This is conveyed in the first sequence of the film, when she arrives on the train and wanders across the platform, looking around warily, unsure of herself. She is in an alien environment in which she does not belong, like a fish out of water. She still cherishes her ideals of what life should be like, but she is not likely to find those ideals fulfilled at the Kowalski home, and she is also very conscious of the different social class to which Stanley belongs. This is another thing that sets her apart from her environment. In contrast, Stanley and Stella seem not only to be happy together but to fit into their environment, a lively, poor area of New Orleans that seems to have a sense of community. All the people there belong where they are; it is Blanche who is the rootless one.

It is because Blanche is so lonely that she reaches out to Mitch, hopeful that perhaps he could be her protector. For a short while it even appears possible, since Mitch is the play's other lonely character. He does not quite fit in. In the film, he is slightly better dressed than the other men in the poker game—he wears a tie—and his manners are more refined. His life is restricted because he has to look after his sick mother. She will soon die, leaving him alone. He courts Blanche, hoping that she might end his loneliness. They are thus drawn to each other by strong mutual need.

Reality

The New Orleans that Blanche finds herself in is a gritty, realistic world. People get on with their lives, doing what they have to do to get by, and they find their enjoyments. Blanche cannot survive in the real world. Her life is the story of one loss after another. She lost her husband a long time ago, and then she lost the family home she had tried so hard to maintain. She managed to stay afloat for a while as a schoolteacher, but her loneliness led her into a foolish relationship with a seventeen-year-old boy. She now has no means of making a living. The real world has defeated her, so she falls back on the one thing that she has, or hopes she still has: her ability as a woman to attract a male protector who will shield her from the harshness of life. This depends on maintaining her appearance, but Blanche is aging, and she knows it. She is obsessed with her appearance, always seeking reassurance about it. The reality is that time is slowly robbing Blanche of her beauty, but this is not something she can accept. She wants to keep up the illusion. She tells Stanley, in a moment of honesty and self-revelation, that "a woman's charm is fifty percent illusion." The more hopeless her life becomes, the more she creates illusions to live by.

READ. WATCH. WRITE.

- Read the final scene of the play and then watch the same scene in the film version. How closely does the film keep to the play? Has the dialogue been cut or otherwise altered? Do the filmmakers follow Williams's detailed stage directions? Write an essay in which you discuss the differences.

- Watch chapter 7 of the film in the DVD selections, and write an essay in which you analyze the contrast between how the women, especially Stella and Blanche, are presented and how the poker-playing men are seen. What does this scene tell you about relations between men and women in the film, and the different values they have?

- Why are there so many closeups in the film and not so many long shots or establishing shots? Why would a director choose a closeup over a longer shot? Select three to five closeups from the film. For each closeup, write a brief paragraph in which you explain the context of the shot and then explain what the actor or actress is conveying in his or her facial expressions.

- With another student, investigate what might be the main differences between a film and a play. What possibilities does film present that are not possible on the stage? From the opposite point of view, what advantages might the stage have over a film? Give a class presentation in which you discuss these issues, using *A Streetcar Named Desire* as an example, emphasizing the places where play and film differ.

- Vivien Leigh and Marlon Brando are both famous for their roles in this film. With another student, analyze the scene (chapter 4 in the DVD selections) in which Blanche meets Stanley for the first time. How does Leigh, through facial expression, gesture, and other means, convey what Blanche is feeling? What do these nonverbal elements suggest about Blanche's state of mind, beyond the words that she actually speaks? Analyze Brando's performance in the same way. What is his attitude toward Blanche in this scene, and how does he convey it through facial expression, gesture, and movement? Give a class presentation in which you first show the scene and then analyze it using a PowerPoint presentation.

When Mitch wants to switch the light on so he can see her properly, she tells him she does not want realism, she wants magic. She wants life transformed, not as it is. She knew love a very long time ago, and it briefly lit up the world for her. She wants to find this transformation again, but it cannot happen. Eventually, her wafer-thin grasp on reality vanishes completely. She retreats into an illusory world in which she is preparing to go on a cruise with a millionaire from Texas. This is her madness: the substitution of a false world for the real one and the inability to tell the difference between the two.

Love

Stanley and Stella have a down-to-earth yet passionate relationship that keeps them bound to each other in a way that Blanche does not understand. As husband and wife, they enjoy a physical intimacy. Blanche is not interested in a relationship based only on physical attraction. The streetcar she takes to reach the Kowalskis' home is appropriately called Desire, but for Blanche desire means the desire for a deeper kind of love, not merely physical. Tragically for Blanche, her desire for true love, for deep connection with another person, is continually being thwarted, and she is associated with what she tells Mitch is the opposite of desire—death. The central event in her life was the death of her husband, and she cannot escape the memory of it. Nor can she forget the many deaths of her relatives at Belle Reve. Reminders of death keep cropping up to pin Blanche back to these dark memories: the inscription on Mitch's cigarette case, for example, given to him by a dying girl, is a quotation from the poet Elizabeth Barrett Browning about love and death. Then the Mexican woman comes to the house selling flowers for funerals. While Stella and Stanley have found a way to keep the flame of life burning, the unhappy Blanche leads an empty, loveless life, which is a kind of death for her, the negation of everything she desires.

Musical Symbolism

The musical score was composed by Alex North, for which he was nominated for an Academy Award. North combined the rhythms and harmonies of jazz with classical orchestral music that has a symphonic dimension. North referred to the music as "simulated jazz," since as written music it lacks the spontaneous quality associated with jazz. (This comment is made by the record producer Robert Townson in the special feature "North and the Music of the South" in the DVD edition of the film.) Townson also comments that North's intention was to create music that reflects the psychological conditions of the characters. All the music is in some way related to the main musical theme that is heard at the beginning of the film. The only exception to this is the French polka music, which is heard every time Blanche is reminded of her dead husband, since this was the tune that the band was playing when her husband shot himself. In the scene in which the young man comes to the apartment for newspaper money, for example, the polka music is heard, which tells the audience, without the need for words, that the young man reminds Blanche of her deceased husband.

In composing the music for the film, North stayed close to the play. Williams, the playwright, describes the music of the "blue piano," coming from the Four Deuces bar, as expressing the spirit of life in that part of New Orleans. The piano music is also heard at times in conjunction with brass, drums, and clarinet, according to the changing mood and atmosphere of the play. The opposite of the piano music, which represents life, is the polka music, also called the Varsouviana music, which represents death.

Montage

After the opening credits, there is a sequence known as a montage, a succession of shots following quickly one after the other to create, in this case, an overall impression of the setting. These are long shots (shots in which the camera is at some distance from the objects) that show the larger environment. First, there is a long shot from the air looking down on the railroad tracks and the steam locomotive. This is followed by a shot from ground level as the camera follows the taxi cabs at night as they head for and arrive at the railroad station as the train pulls in. Then there is a busy shot of people emerging from the waiting room to greet arriving travelers. As the camera pans to the left, we see Blanche emerging surrounded by steam from the locomotive. The montage has moved from the general (the busy urban setting) to the particular (the main character) in just a few shots.

Visual Symbolism

Film has an advantage over the stage in that it presents possibilities for creating visual images that tell the story of what happens without words or even showing the action itself. An example of this visual symbolism occurs toward the end of the film. As Stanley approaches Blanche with aggressive intent, the film cuts to a shot of a smashed mirror. This shot suggests, without actually showing it, that Blanche has thrown the broken bottle at Stanley and missed, but more important, it conveys symbolically that Blanche herself is shattered by this last encounter with her brother-in-law. She is as fragile as glass and she eventually breaks. The symbol of the broken mirror tells this story in a few seconds, without words.

Censorship

When the film was made in 1951, standards of what was considered acceptable for mass entertainment were different from what they are today. Although it was an extremely successful stage play, *A Streetcar Named Desire* also had a reputation for containing some sensational and morally questionable material. When the film was made, it had to be approved by the Motion Picture Production Code, popularly known as the Hays Code, after its founder, Will H. Hays. In order that the film might be deemed suitable for family viewing, several scenes had to be slightly rewritten in order to satisfy the censors. In the play, for example, Blanche's husband commits suicide because he is troubled by his homosexuality and Blanche's negative response to it. In those days, homosexuality was considered a shameful thing, and the filmmakers were not permitted to include any reference to it.

Another change demanded by the censors was that Stanley should be punished for his assault on Blanche at the end of the play. Therefore, in the film, Stella vows that she will never go back to Stanley; however, in the play, Stanley comforts Stella, who is upset over the fact that she has committed Blanche to a mental institution. There is no suggestion that Stanley and Stella will split up.

Other small cuts had to be made to satisfy the Legion of Decency, a Catholic organization that had a rating system for films. Originally, the Legion advised Warner Brothers that *A Streetcar Named Desire* would receive a C rating from them, which meant that it would be deemed a morally unsuitable film for Catholics to see. Not wanting to have people discouraged from seeing the film, Warner was ready to compromise, so twelve more cuts, amounting to four minutes of screen time, were made. These cuts included part of the scene in which Stella descends a staircase to Stanley, who waits below. The close-ups and medium shots of Stella were considered too suggestive of Stella's physical attraction to Stanley—the fact that Stanley and Stella are husband and wife seems not to have made any difference to the Legion-so a long shot was substituted in which the expression on Stella's face could not be seen. The changes mollified the Legion of Decency, which issued the film a B rating. This meant that it had some objectionable material, but the revised rating meant that theaters would not be put off from showing it. The director of the film, Elia Kazan, was not happy with the changes that were forced on him, believing that they compromised the artistic integrity of the film. Tennessee Williams also expressed the idea that the ending of the film was unsatisfactory.

In 1993, some of the material that was cut from the original film was restored. This restored version runs a few minutes longer than the 122 minutes of the 1951 film, and is the version that is commercially available on DVD.

Method Acting

As Stanley Kowalski, Marlon Brando brought a new method of acting to Hollywood. This was Method acting, which Brando had studied at the Dramatic Workshop of the New School in New York City, where he was coached by Stella Adler in the methods of the Russian theater director, Konstanin Stanislavski (1863-1938). Another acting teacher associated with popularizing Method acting in the United States was Lee Strasberg (1901-1982). Method actors sought to gain a new depth, intensity, and authenticity to their work by recalling emotional experiences in their own lives, and using other techniques, to understand and represent the emotions of the characters they were portraying. In *A Streetcar Named Desire*, Brando's Method acting contrasted with that of Vivien Leigh, who was trained in the classical British acting style. Method acting became extremely popular in the United States in the 1940s and 1950s, in part due to the success of Brando and James Dean, another Method actor.

Critical Overview

A Streetcar Named Desire was an immediate success at the box office, and it also garnered twelve Academy Award nominations. The reviewer for *Look* accurately assesses the quality of the film: "*Streetcar* now seizes a place among Hollywood's rare great movies" (quoted in Philip C. Kolin's *Williams: A Streetcar Named Desire*), although the film was also denounced in some quarters as immoral and shocking.

Now over fifty years old, the film has stood the test of time. A new wave of interest in it was created by the restoration in 1993 of several minutes that had been cut in the original 1951 version. Roger Ebert reviewed the restored version of the film for the *Chicago Sun-Times*. After commenting on how the restored parts are crucial to the play's meaning and that Brando's style of acting was soon to dominate Hollywood films, Ebert also notes how suitable the film is to black-and-white photography. "Color would have been fatal to the special tone. It would have made the characters seem too real, when we need them exactly like this, black and gray and silver, shadows projected on the screens of their own dreams and needs."

In 2008, when the film was presented as part of a Williams season at London's BFI Southbank, Peter Bradshaw wrote in the London *Guardian* that "Brando is lethally powerful," although he was less impressed with Vivien Leigh's "stagey, mad-eyed performance, often pitilessly inspected in close-up."

In 2007, the film was ranked forty-fifth in a list of the hundred greatest American films by the American Film Institute.

Sources

"AFI's 100 Years ... The Complete Lists," in *American Film Institute*, http://connect.afi.com/site/PageServer? pagename=100YearsList (accessed June 22, 2009).

Bradshaw, Peter, Review of *A Streetcar Named Desire*, in *Guardian* (London, England), November 14, 2008, http://www.guardian.co.uk/film/2008/nov/14/streetc; named-desire-film-review (accessed June 22, 2009).

Ebert, Roger, Review of *A Streetcar Named Desire*, in *Chicago SunTimes*, November 12, 1993, http://rogerebert.suntimes.com/apps/pbcs.dll/article? AID=/19931112/REVIEWS/311120304/1023 (accessed June 22, 2009).

Kolin, Philip C., *Williams: A Streetcar Named Desire*, Cambridge University Press, 2000, p. 151.

Schvey, Henry I., "Madonna at the Poker Night: Pictorial Elements in Tennessee Williams's *A Streetcar Named Desire*," in *Tennessee Williams's "A Streetcar Named Desire,"* edited and with an introduction by Harold Bloom, Chelsea House, 1988, p. 108.

Williams, Tennessee, *A Streetcar Named Desire*, New American Library, 1947.

CPSIA information can be obtained
at www.ICGtesting.com
Printed in the USA
LVHW090559291018
595170LV00013B/274/P

9 781375 398985